Skull

Amy Baskin

A Publication of The Poetry Box®

Poems © 2024 Amy Baskin
All rights reserved

Editing & Book Design by Shawn Aveningo Sanders
Cover Art by Jason Baskin
Author Photo by Eric Patton

Skull was a finalist in The Poetry Box Chapbook Prize 2024

No part of this book may be republished without permission from the author, except in the case of brief quotations embodied in critical essays, epigraphs, reviews and articles, or publisher/author's marketing collateral.

ISBN: 978-1-956285-80-2
Published in the United States of America
Wholesale Distribution by Ingram Group

Published by The Poetry Box, December 2024
Portland, Oregon, United States
website: ThePoetryBox.com

Dedicated to my healthcare givers:

Susan Vockert-Burke, FNP; Dr. Macson Lee, OD, FCOVD; Cresaya E. Kingsbury, M.A., O.V.T.; Dr. Heidi Olejnik, DC; Kurt Marion, LMT; and Lynn Emmons, LCSW, RN, CADCI

Thank you for your big hearts, your deep listening, and for teaching me ways to heal.

Contents

- 9 ⋄ Unseated
- 11 ⋄ After the Crash
- 12 ⋄ What I Know Every Time We Get Behind the Wheel
- 13 ⋄ Visual Disturbance
- 14 ⋄ On Darkness
- 16 ⋄ Scintillant
- 17 ⋄ Sulk-Stained
- 18 ⋄ *Sella Turcica*
- 19 ⋄ Aunt Beast
- 20 ⋄ Backbone
- 21 ⋄ Bare and Brave
- 22 ⋄ Needy
- 23 ⋄ Trailing Breadcrumbs
- 24 ⋄ Breast Exam During the Pandemic
- 25 ⋄ Kansas Isn't Kansas Anymore
- 27 ⋄ Desiccant
- 28 ⋄ "If you want the rainbow"
- 29 ⋄ lace up your shoes already
- 30 ⋄ Love Note to My First… Dose of Pfizer
- 31 ⋄ Baby Girl
- 32 ⋄ Fall Down Seven Times, Get Up Eight

- 35 ⋄ Acknowledgments
- 37 ⋄ About the Author

Skull (noun)
1. The skeleton of the head of a vertebrate forming a bony or cartilaginous case that encloses and protects the brain and chief sense organs and supports the jaws.
2. The seat of understanding or intelligence: mind. See also "out of one's skull."

Skull (transitive verb)
1. To hit on the head

—from the *Merriam-Webster Dictionary*

UNSEATED

~a view from an impairment

what do I need to do now
where is the glove composite
compostment department
the grill the hood the bumper look like

a music machine
what's it called it's an
armament an instructment
a musical fold

head rests on the seat
shock through my arms trunk legs
slows at my neck
fuel is leaking from me

a slow drip
under the mind my
engine is unseated
it lost its upgrade

help me I am off
I was here and now I'm here
let me just think for a minute
th nk fo a m n t

I think can I think
is this thinking
start the thing
move the accardion

see my face and body
exit the driver door
not a scrape
bruise or break

what did that
other driver
just say
iam glaad yer okei

After the Crash

~a concussed ballade

Shock starts in one eye
then flutters through the brain.
A drunken butterfly
that must be retrained.
It jolts down the thigh,
charges the whole neural map,
floods a cerebral vein,
and the only help is to nap.

Search for arnica to apply
and pills to ease the pain.
Every salve to try
requires patience. Explain
the floating slosh of images. The refrain
of electric ideas behind the eyelids that zap
all strength. It must sound mundane
that the only help is to nap.

Envision this head. Go on—try.
A fat, jostled lump with a stain.
The jellied grey folds to rely
on—bruised birds striking windowpanes.
Smile in conversation. Feign
understanding of mouths that flap.
Words pelt the skull like pounding rain
and the only help is to nap.

Let this fragile membrane
regain all its sap—
its plasma both sanguine and profane.
Lay in the darkness and nap.

What I Know Every Time We Get Behind the Wheel

~to my sister, who wasn't as lucky

Stars tunnel, vision to black. Heads don't
even need to hit dashboards, the adverse
ramming his SUV into the passenger side.

Once, heart pulsed in the belly. Now, liquid
spurts from tailpipe, windows, veins, and
eyes.

I am here because two kids made the drive back
from Pike's Peak with a wine-stained picnic blanket
and high blood-alcohol content.

I was handed my own set of car keys when I
turned sixteen, before I had even changed
out of my pjs.

At some church, a lilac tree is forever planted in
your name. By the Flatirons, we dressed a bench
with a plaque, before you had even graduated.

Visual Disturbance

The air is salted, tingling
in a red way

through the porthole, light projects
on my eyelids.

What sea bird pecks through
my mind, prodding pain,

nesting in the knuckle of my fisted skull,
scratching hatch marks

on ganglion ropes? I cannot summon
the spell to shoo it.

And when it flutters
away on its own accord,

and I scrub my galley clean
of feathers and droppings,

it homes back
through the wine-dark sea.

On Darkness

I must be honest with you here about my own life. For the last ten years, I have had little spiritual feeling, neither consolation, nor desolation.
—Father Richard Rohr

    Today's been one
    of these days
    these flatlining days.

    These darkness days
    in the Kansas of my mind,
    all sepia tone,

    from the ginger ale
    to the bourbon, no
    technicolor or fresh limes.

    No negative,
    just no positive, either.
    No pain, just no feeling.

    These days, I have
    to rely upon memory.
    The recognition

    that there is blue sky—
    open, ignorant above
    the padded cloud cover

    that diffuses light
    and dark and lends,
    with no interest,

the world gradients
of grey with no depth,
no shadow.

Scintillant

"Vintage" Edison LED bulbs sear my eyes and brain
to the point where I need medication to function and
sunglasses to navigate my way through the living
world, the living room.

My partner knows me. Knows that I will take months
to decide upon paint chips and upholstery fabric,

knows that I prefer the dark with a smattering of
seasonal lights strung along the mantle with few lumens,

and he thinks he understands why, though it bothers him
that I am not moved by his need for brightness.

He thinks he knows me, but he cannot know me.
He cannot see through my eyes, and though truly

I wish I could, I cannot escape my head and settle
comfortably behind the ridge of his forehead, either.

Current top relationship experts insist we should not know
everything about each other. Leave the candle of mystery lit.

Learn everything and risk dousing all the flames of passion.
Lean in too close and risk smoldering that flame.

I say fine to all this. Let's give our candle plenty of air.
May it burn hot, but—can we cover it with a lampshade?

Sulk-Stained

Ponder the skull paperweight
on the physician's desk, again.

Alas, you'll be poor Yorick soon enough;
why choose now?

Take your medication like you wish your loved ones would
and savor each day.

Stop steeping in low-grade tea dust thoughts.
Sweep those away.

SELLA TURCICA

~for Dr. Heidi Olejnik, DC

In my skull,
a butterfly bone
flutters, restless,

slipped saddle
to lobes
and glands.

She registers distress
reading the skull's
cryptic Braille.

Her hands
harness.
Replace on rails

this drawer
that moments ago
would not shut.

Now
will it hold
my thoughts?

Sella Turcica: part of the sphenoid, a compound bone that forms the base of the cranium, behind the eye and below the front part of the brain.

Aunt Beast

Life, with its rules, its obligations, and its freedoms, is like a sonnet: You're given the form, but you have to write the sonnet yourself.
　　　　　—Mrs. Whatsit, *A Wrinkle in Time*
　　　　　　by Madeline L'Engle

You found me hurt. You drew me to your chest
and saw me as I was, though you are blind.
You covered me in fur and gave me rest.
My body, hard as stone, sensed you were kind.
You spoke through tentacles that held my cheek.
Relaxed the frigid stiffness of my fear.
And though my father thinks I am too weak,
I have to rescue Charles. To us, it's clear.
Your music taught me grace and I won't quit.
I'll live this love, more tangible than form,
and rescue my dear Charles from that thief, It.
Your song emboldens me to face this storm.
You know the Black Thing burns, and how we grieve.
Goodbye, Aunt Beast. Now, sing me how to leave.

Backbone

metal rods installed
to scaffold each shattered vertebra
calcified, chalky thoughts
ground to dust, propped up
by bookshelves full
of the way things ought to be
rigid, immovable discs dissolve
height shifts inches shorter
losing ground on the beachhead

watch the contortionist flip
a spine is a fish
releasing itself from each
net and line
cousin to thick stands of bamboo
whose tops bend and touch ground,
blown by tsunami yet
as telephone poles snap and collapse,
that grass never breaks

let minds bend, make ideas
take a pounding
see if they can spring back up
reformed in unexpected designs
let cores nurture each newborn
soft dough, rolled and stretched out
shaped into dumplings
pliant and tractable
willing

Bare and Brave

supine
waiting for warmth

for the effete blues
to turn to action

but for now recumbent
a fungal outcropping

at the root of
a barren trunk

do humors
circulate through me

what gives me the
strength to move

through this rectangular
world, angling for

signs of greenery
the flush of a sexed

winterberry clustered
on a twig

asymmetry to muscle
me forth and back again

Needy

*~a villanelle for the one who
taught me it's ok to need help*

On mornings when the sun can't find me
through the clouds amidst the grey
I find the one who sleeps beside me

watch him breathe and let him be
my lover at the break of day
on mornings when the sun can't find me.

Under covers, he lays dreaming
soon he'll leave, to my dismay.
I spoon the one who sleeps beside me—

wrap my arms around him, wondering
why he still decides to stay
on mornings when the sun can't find me

when my mood feels paralyzing
he wakes and prods me into play.
I find the one who sleeps beside me

brighter than that solar orb, glowing
warmth, he radiates and lights my way
on mornings when the sun can't find me
I thank the one who sleeps beside me.

Trailing Breadcrumbs

The mail carrier is young and attractive.
I did not know this until today, sitting on
my porch. He walked slowly up our stairs,
considering the lilies. Three crows followed
him, hopping up the vaulted lawn.

You have some adoring fans, I told him.
I make friends wherever I walk just in case
I need to turn back, he explained,
and showed me his handful of feed, which he
scattered and they retrieved.

Just like you, when you took a wrong turn
in Vancouver and found yourself in an alley
between Chinatown and Gastown, where sick
people were sharing needles. These days,
we should all carry extra unused ones

to hand out everywhere we go, you told me.
You heard that street had so many needles,
the birds there used them to build their nests.
You chose another route back to your hotel,
searching for somewhere to buy Narcan.

Breast Exam During the Pandemic

Some years I joke with my doctor
about the intimacy of the act.
Are those your cold, palpating hands
or are you just happy to feel me?

Sometimes the intimacy of the act
is no joke when she says
my breasts are fibrous
and uncooperative.

This year, the intimacy of the act
is not buffered by blue comedy
or exposed to threatening news.
It's just that

over the past year,
she's the first person
out of my household
who has touched me.

Kansas Isn't Kansas Anymore

It creeps up on you. One morning
you look down on the floor
next to your bed and notice

that someone shed
a matronly undergarment there
and that someone was you.

You had ordered it without realizing
that shade of beige, that elastic texture,
that shapewear

would look anything other
than sexy as it had on that
buxom young model online.

On you, it looks like it has been
hanging on a clothesline
traumatized in a twister.

Once crisp, tinged sepia now,
back from Oz, apart from
your Scarecrow love, heels clicking,

you find you can never return.
You are no longer Dorothy.
You are firmly Auntie Em.

The farmhands no longer notice you.
They're all fawning over your daughter
in your childhood bed.

She's asleep.
She's running a fever,
but she hasn't coughed yet.

"Her collar looks tight,"
one observes.
"Should we loosen it at the neck?"

You tell him to skedaddle.
To keep his distance.
You wet a washcloth.

Help her body cool. You fashion a mask
out of the old undergarment
based on a YouTube tutorial.

You're all out of wishes. If someone claimed
your house had dropped from the sky,
you would believe it.

Desiccant

*Climate Fires, 2020.
Air Quality Index 450,
Portland, Oregon.*

Shove my body in a bottle.
I'll keep your drugs dry.

Dehydrated jerky.
Unused kitchen sponge.

Depleted.
Drained in a corner.

Waiting for rain.
Waiting for the wash away.

When will we reckon
with the wreckage?

The wasteland
outside our door?

"If you want the rainbow"

—Dolly Parton's infinitely wise words

"The way I see it, if you want the rainbow
you gotta put up with the rain."
But storms can hit harder than any blow.

Just when you need relief, the skies will flow
and pummel you with tears and aches and pain.
The way I see it, if you want the rainbow,

kiss your hurts and hug them close. Above all, take it slow.
And breathe! Losing your shit cannot be called "a gain;"
your storms can hit harder than any blow!

Get wet. Jump in puddles toe-to-toe.
Take a stroll, hand-in-hand with a friend. This is sane.
The way I see it, if you want the rainbow,

thank the rain! It saturates you 'til you know
you cannot get any wetter. Head inside. Get dry again
once storms have hit harder than any blow.

Towel off. Drink tea. Cuddle. Then work hard! And throw
aside the fears that you can't take it. Let those wane.
The way I see it, if you want the rainbow,
know storms hit hard. They're part of getting clean and letting go.

LACE UP YOUR SHOES ALREADY

tendons shrunken, muscles bound, soft tissue pain
bones creaking, breaking, shattering in shards now
fifty reasons for not running in the rain
regimens fixed and promised, a solemn vow
days without discipline welt like water stains
candy coated flour dredged cortex allows
all sorts of ideas that shouldn't be thought
chase them away before they stick and get caught

Love Note to My First...
Dose of Pfizer

Though I didn't feel like mentioning it
to my friends or online acquaintances
with their purity politics,

it was, in fact, a deep source
of happiness. I couldn't—didn't—wait
to put you inside me.

Lying there, marinating with you,
you tenderized me. I imagined you
coursing through my veins,

unzipping my RNA
like a 17 year-old male
under the bleachers.

Faster than you'd expect—
then slowing down and waiting
for your wing man

that second dose—
to show you how to unroll
protection.

Baby Girl

And when the news pinned me down in bed,
I dared myself to write a list: three things I valued.

Faith, hope, and charity. Those were three.
My pen kept moving. My hand continued: love and peace.

Then peace, a calm I felt myself there—
then love, a furnace, pumped heat from core to fingertips,

urging me to write down names of friends,
then things we've done together, spanning four continents,

which made me think of the unmet friends—
possibilities awaiting us all today and every day.

I yawned and stretched, Got out of bed
and went to soak in a silent pool of potential.

A baby bathed there with her mama.
We talked for half an hour without making a sound.

Her eyes and energy met my own. When she smiled, I smiled.
When she stopped, I stopped. And waited.

I met her, splash for splash. We giggled.
Thank you, baby girl, for bringing me out of my head.

Fall Down Seven Times, Get Up Eight

Cobwebs from October's spiders
still festoon the corners of my rooms.
I could take a broom and a wet rag to them
right now, but that requires more effort.

I could ask someone else to do it, but I haven't yet.
Most people I know wait for the first spring buds
as signs of hope, while today's clouds
diffuse light and leave no room for shadow,

all of us vampiring around. The furnace is groaning
its death rattle. It has lost the strength to heat.
I started today with a list of ten "must-do's,"
and I've finished part of one and then napped for an hour

because that single effort took all day.
But—allow me to bear witness to the kindness of each obstacle.
This morning, walking past neighbors,
stubbing my trick toe on an eighth inch of raised sidewalk,

I thought to curse the homeowner who hasn't yet repaired
the path, but I got up instead. I stopped, held my foot
for a moment, smiled, and thanked the pain with breath.
And later this afternoon, while calling roofers to fix an attic leak,

I got on my knees, bowed down to the stained,
soaked plaster, and acknowledged my generous teacher, adversity,
mymost constant mentor, whom I can always count on to find me.
I want ease, sunlight, and elections won handily by good people.

I want prepared meals and love to hunt me down and lift me up out
from the storm cellar. But sometimes, waking, I know this steady diet
of monotony and defeat might nourish me. I place my bare feet
on the wooden floor, catch a splinter in the meat of my heel,

and I'm startled by the truth—true as anything I've learned:
each gremlin, spanner in the works, sabotage of my best-laid plans
is a summoner, a child vying for my attention, insisting there is still time
to notice that I am bleeding again, yet standing up, persistent, and alive.

Acknowledgments

I gratefully acknowledge the editors of the publications in which these poems first appeared, sometimes in different versions:

Amethyst Review: "If you want the rainbow"

Bear Review: "Unseated" and "Visual Disturbance"

Gobshite Quarterly: "What I Know Every Time We Get Behind the Wheel" and "Scintillant"

Literary Mama: "Kansas Isn't Kansas Anymore"

Please See Me: "Sella Turcica"

Postcard Poems & Prose: "lace up your shoes already"

The Literary Nest: "Aunt Beast"

Visual Verse: "Backbone" and "Bare and Brave"

About the Author:

Amy Baskin is a Pushcart Prize and Best of the Net nominee, an Oregon Literary Arts Fellow, and an Oregon Poetry Association prizewinner. Her work can be found in anthologies and journals including the *HOCUS Tarot, Pirene's Fountain, Friends Journal*, and *SWWIM*. When not writing, she works for the Departments of English and History at Lewis & Clark College and helps run literary arts programs including Fir Acres Writing Workshop. She is the author of *Hysterical Cake* (Dancing Girl Press, 2021), *Night Hag* (Unsolicited Press, 2023).

About The Poetry Box®

The Poetry Box, a boutique publishing company in Portland, Oregon, provides a platform for both established and emerging poets to share their words with the world through beautiful printed books and chapbooks.

Feel free to visit the online bookstore (thePoetryBox.com), where you'll find more titles including:

metal used for beauty alone by Claudia F. Saleeby Savage

Exhanging Wisdom by Christopher & Angelo Luna

Now Is What Matters by Janet Steward

Blue Chip Stamp Guitar by Sue Fagalde Lick

Vitals & Other Signs of Life by David A. Goodrum

gOD: A Respectfully Divergent Testament by Penelope Scambly Schott

When All Else Fails by Lana Hechtman Ayers

Earthwork by Kristin Berger

A Nest in the Heart by Vivienne Popperl

This Is the Lightness by Rachel Barton

Self Dissection by Amelia Diaz Ettinger

Listening in the Dark by Suzy Harris

Transition Thunderstorms by Beth Bonness

and more . . .

www.ingramcontent.com/pod-product-compliance
Lightning Source LLC
LaVergne TN
LVHW050028080526
838202LV00069B/6959